WHAT IS A KUMQUAT?

What Is
a Kumquat?

and other poems

SUE COWLING

Illustrated by
Gunvor Edwards

faber and faber
LONDON · BOSTON

First published in 1991
by Faber and Faber Limited
3 Queen Square London WC1N 3AU

Photoset by Wilmaset, Birkenhead, Wirral
Printed in Great Britain by
Cox & Wyman Ltd, Reading, Berkshire

A CIP record for this book is
available from the British Library

ISBN 0 571 16065 4

2 4 6 8 10 9 7 5 3

For Rachel and Chris

Contents

Today

Today I wrote a letter,
I wrote it on a stone.
I rolled it down the mountain-side
And let it lie alone.

Today I wrote a story,
I wrote it on a kite.
I flew it for the wind to read
And let it out of sight.

Today I wrote a poem,
I rowed it out to sea.
I fed it to a shark who seemed
More interested in ME!

Leaves

My wellingtons swish
through the leaves.
I am four years old again, at play
in the crumpled wrapping paper
of the year.

Houses

Where would you live if you were me?
A lonely lighthouse in the sea
With a garden of waves and rocks?
A narrowboat nosing through locks?
A windmill with a winding stair
And round rooms stacked like building blocks –
Would you live there?

Where would I live if I were you?
A wooden ark, a floating zoo.
A swaying eyrie in a tree
Would do for me.
An igloo with an icy dome,
A painted gypsy caravan,
A paper palace in Japan
Could be my home.

Marjorie

She was short-sighted and wore glasses.
She was a Sunday School teacher.
She was engaged to a soldier.
She had her picture taken in a grey dress.
She died at twenty-one of scarlet fever.
She was buried on Christmas Eve.
This is all I know about her,
The aunt I never knew, my mother's sister.
Is it my face or hers in the mirror?
Her face or mine in the frame?
And whom do they see when they look at me?

Old Gillow

Old Gillow
skin sallow
cheeks hollow
eyes yellow
can't swallow
breath shallow
pains follow
poor fellow!

Migration

Such a
chirping
whistling
rustling
and jostling
merry-making
leave-taking
party in a tree!
Off they go
with a clap of wings –
Goodbye, goodbye,
goodbye till Spring.

Nicholas

Nicholas, Nicholas, Nicholas Lane,
You drive me bananas, you drive me insane.
Your trousers are ripped and your tie's round your ear,
Your pockets weren't made for your hands, is that clear?
You still haven't tucked in the tails of your shirt,
Your shoelaces dangle from shoes thick with dirt.
Don't say you can't help it, I know that you can.
You'd better turn over a new leaf, young man!

Nicholas, Nicholas, Nicholas, think –
You'll get someone worse if you drive me to drink.
You switch off completely and gaze into space.
You break all the pencils, get ink on your face.
Your exercise book looks as if it's been chewed.
You slouch and you swear, you're defiant and rude –
When I see your parents where shall I begin?
Now why were you blessed with that wonderful grin?

Have I Got Everything?

Have I got everything
I'll need today?
Art folder
cookery basket
lunchbox
clarinet
needlework
P.E. kit
hockey stick –
Daren't forget
pencil case
calculator
science overall –
Is that the lot?
Or should I take
my mac in case it's wet?
I feel a bit unladylike
but never mind –
Now, where's my bike?

Ten Syllables for Spring

daffylonglegs
blowing
buttered trumpets

Snowstorm Haiku

like being inside
a kaleidoscope where all
the patterns are white

Song of the Victorian Mine

Shut six men in a metal cage –
    Wind them down, wind them down.
Drop them in a dismal pit –
    Down in the mine,
    Deep in the mine,
    Dark in the mine all day.

Back the pony up to the cage –
    Wind him down, wind him down.
Trip him up and make him sit –
    Down in the mine,
    Deep in the mine,
    Dark in the mine all day.

Load the ore in the metal cage –
    Wind it down, wind it down.
Waterlogged and candlelit –
    Down in the mine,
    Deep in the mine,
    Dark in the mine all day.

Bring the canary in his cage –
    Wind him down, wind him down.
He'll die first if the air's not fit –
    Down in the mine,
    Deep in the mine,
    Dark in the mine all day.

Thirty thousand times in the cage –
    Wind me down, wind me down.
Fill my lungs with grime and grit –
    Down in the mine,
    Deep in the mine,
    Dark in the mine all day.

Quiet Things

Hush! I'll show you quiet things –
moon and stars and a barn owl's wings
speckled moth on mottled sill
white mare standing paper-still
gap-toothed gravestones, hollow trees
flat-roofed fungus colonies
coins and bones long buried deep
hedgehog hunched in spiny sleep.

Country Carol

Walked on the crusted grass in the frosty air.
Blackbird saw me, gave me a gold-rimmed stare.

Walked in the winter woods where the snow lay deep.
Hedgehog heard me, smiled at me in his sleep.

Walked by the frozen pond where the ice shone pale.
Wind sang softly, moon dipped its silver sail.

Walked on the midnight hills till the star-filled dawn.
No one told me, I knew a king was born.

Practising

I've been practising
Snapping cucumbers in half
Like our veg man
In his veg van.
I watch him every Friday.

First he glares at them,
Then when he's sure they're still
He cracks his wrists down,
Splits

The juicy flesh, the seeds and skin
Dead-centre.
His
Is always a clean break.
(Mine are a bit ragged!)

Perhaps one day
I'll be as good as him.
Till then I'd best get practising again.

Postal Strike

Letterboxes gagged
with wooden blocks
gob-stoppered
empty-bellied hostages
hungry for contact
with the outside world
functions suspended
prisoners of time
from within
a black and silent shout
a prayer
Good Lord deliver us!

Lechwe

We're sure
they really think
they're birds!

They spend most of the day
with us
the pelicans, ibis, herons and ducks
eating the same weed
wading the same marsh
cooling their hooves
in a docile and sensible way

Then suddenly – they lay
their horns along their backs
and take off
bucking, bounding through the swamp
they scatter spray
and leap aloft
trailing their legs as they have seen us do

We're sad to see them go
strung out on the horizon like a frieze
although we're sure
they really think
they're birds!

The Elephant Child

Under an African sun he stands,
the elephant child,
hot and hungry and thirsty.
He's as big as a car
but still small for an elephant.
Sadly swinging his trunk he stands
for many hours beside his mother,
trying to coax and nudge her back to life
to take him home.
He could not help her when the men came.
They just laughed at him.
And now
under an African moon he stands
and tries to make sense of her butchered face.
Then he cries as only an elephant can cry
but he does not understand.
Neither do I.

Jeopardy

'You know his job's in Jeopardy,'
I heard them say when I was small.
Where was it? I imagined it
all jungly and leopardy
with butterflies like aeroplanes
above a waterfall
which leapt with rainbows, tumbling
to swell a boulder-studded stream.
I roared with it, I raced with it,
we set the canyons rumbling.
He lost his job, and Jeopardy
became a childhood dream.

Sickening

He's always kicking things
my brother
stones
the back gate
me when Mum can't see

He's always flicking things
my brother
crumbs
ink pellets
cold peas from his plate

He's always picking things
my brother
scabs
his toenails
worst of all, his nose

And if it's none of those
he's
tricking me
mimicking me
nicking what belongs to me
never sticking up for me

He's sickening
my brother.

Waiting

In the dentist's waiting room I'm
        nervid
        wunxious
        fothered
        anxit
        weeful
        wobbered
        tummled
        glumpit
        frettled
        horrish
        gumshot
        dismy
        squawbid
        grimlip
        dregless –
        IT'S ME!

The Man on the Stairs

Who's the man on the stairs, Mummy?
I saw him again today.
He tried to catch me by the arm
But his hand melted away.

Why does he seem so sad, Mummy?
He always stands and stares.
His eyes have a funny empty look
And they're such strange clothes he wears.

He says we've met before, Mummy,
Although I'm not sure how.
Sometimes I hear him calling me . . .
Look, Mummy, he's there now.

Litter

Too old for kittens, not yet cats – cattens perhaps, or
    kits?

Matilda, the most cunning, hunts with eyes like watch-
    tower slits.
O'Sullivan, the fighter, opens out his claws and spits
At Clarence chasing round and round as if he'd lost his
    wits,
While mischief-maker Millicent unpicks what Grandma
    knits
And spiteful Wilhelmina tears a butterfly to bits.

But Williams, who's the wisest and the cleverest, just
    . . . sits.

Funny How She Forgets

Funny how she forgets
Her P.E. kit on Mondays –
Not on Fridays when it's gym,
Not on Wednesdays when they swim
Monday is hockey with Mrs Betts –
Funny how she forgets.

Requiem for a Robin

Our mother let us deal with it ourselves.
She swore she'd never have another cat.
We chose a spot beneath the apple tree
Directly underneath the branch he sat
And carolled on. We thought he would approve.
It's hard to say exactly how it felt
To take a spade and dig our friend a grave.
We smoothed his feathers down and then I knelt
To place him in the ground. He looked so small
Compared to when he overflowed with song.
I shuddered when I covered him with earth
And hoped his mate would not grieve for too long.
We sang no hymns, but knew he would be heard
Where lamb lies down with lion, cat with bird.

The Bribe

After exams –
You can do it all then.
You can visit your friends,
You can stay out till ten.

After exams
You can do as you like.
You can play table-tennis,
Dismantle your bike,

Spend the day at the swimming-pool,
Hang round the shops,
You can fool with the dog
And watch *Top of the Pops*.

After exams
We may even allow
The party you mentioned –
But please, revise NOW!

L

I shan't forget that little villain, L,
Who plagued me for a year in Class 4C.
She used to take delight in raising hell.

Her name I won't reveal – it's just as well
To hide the dreadful child's identity.
I shan't forget that little villain, L.

The fire-alarm went off – she rang the bell
After she locked me in the lavatory.
She used to take delight in raising hell.

The day we went pond-dipping, in she fell!
She couldn't swim, though I could, luckily.
I shan't forget that little villain, L.

She let the gerbils out – they ran pell-mell.
Miss Pringle ended up in Casualty.
She used to take delight in raising hell.

Although she was a problem, truth to tell,
I missed her when she ran away to sea.
I shan't forget that little villain, L.
She used to take delight in raising hell.

Recipe for a Class Outing

Ingredients:
30 children, washed and scrubbed
29 packed lunches (no bottles)
3 teachers
an equal quantity of mums
1 nosebleed
2 fights
a hot day
3 lost purses
1 slightly torn dress
plenty of sweets
5 or 6 songs (optional)

Method:
Place children and adults in a bus and heat slowly.
Season well with sweets, reserving a few for later.
Heat to boiling point. Add fights and nosebleed.
Leave to simmer for 2 hours.
Remove children and packed lunches and leave to cool.
Stir in torn dress and lost purses.
Return to heat, add songs to taste.
Mix thoroughly. If the children go soggy and start to stick together, remove from the bus and drain.
At the end of the cooking time divide into individual portions (makes about 36).
Serve with relief, garnished liberally with dirt.

The Creek

Metallic jink of rigging in the wind
A shingle shore
The smell of mud and ooze
A torn sky patched by clouds
The squealing cries
Of hungry gulls
The waking boats
That bob and rise
As the creek fills.

Excavator

Flamingo bucket
dipping
sipping
sand and shale.

God Remembers His First Tree

(An adaptation from a French poem by Jules Supervielle)

When I think back to my first tree
it was nothing like I expected,
so many branches took me by surprise –
it was a thousand times a tree.
Each thing I make is part of me
but I had no idea that I had leaves –
yet there I was providing shade
and there were birds all over me.
I hid myself within the sap
of the stately trunk raised to the sky
but I was earth-bound by my roots
and held in nature's gentle trap.
It was about the time of my first tree
that man sat down beneath its shade,
he was still tender and new-made.
Was it an oak tree or an elm?
I'm not sure now, it's been so long
but I know the man was pleased with it
and he went to sleep with his eyes aglow

to dream of a little wood. And so
when he woke from his pleasant nap
I made a forest at one go
with trees a century old
and the three hundred stags that galloped there
with their does and young ones were all sure
they had lived in the forest a very long time,
the six-tined males with their belling call
were the unborn fawns of a moment ago.
With more than their share of hope they sprang forth,
their minds full of memories grown from my own.
There and then I made oaks and firs,
hordes of squirrels to people the treetops,
the child who wanders from the path
and the woodcutter to show him the way.
I hid the sky as best I could
to make its vastness less daunting
but I gave it back as best I could
in the form of birds and the dew of morning.

Moon (i)

bright   still   clean   high
porthole in the morning sky

high   clean   still   bright
space-explorer's traffic-light

still   bright   high   clean
loop-the-lunar trampoline

clean   high   bright   still
gift on morning's windowsill

Moon (ii)

you
  spume-thrower
    wave-stretcher
      foam-snatcher
        spray-raiser
        surf-slinger
      string-puller
    scene-shifter
  tide-turner
moon

Weedy Riddles

Chin up?
(– Buttercup.)
Loves me?
(– Daisy.)
Rainy spell?
(– Pimpernel.)
Wet the bed?
(– Enough said!)

Late-Night Caller

The tick of the clock,
the click of the lock,
a shoeless sock
on the stair,

the groan of the floor,
the squeak of a door,
the sigh of a drawer –
who's there?

A current of air,
a pencil of light –
'I'm back, son. All right?
Goodnight!'

Faces

I find faces
in peculiar places,
staring out of patterns
on the carpet in the hall.
I see the features
of mythical creatures
peering from the flowery paper
on the bedroom wall.

Old banana skin,
peelings in the bin,
look just like the teachers
who can really make you shrink.
Keep your eyes on
the clouds on the horizon,
they can turn to monks or punks
before you blink.

Faces show up
even when you grow up,
crumpled paper bags
look like your boss or an M.P.
I'm amazed at
the faces to be gazed at . . .
What I'd like to know is
can the faces see me?

Hayfever

Pollen
Makes my nose wrinkle
And my eyes pinkle –
Lucky for me
I'm not a bee!

What *Is* a Kumquat?

I'll bet you it's – a sailing ship
an oriental lord
a piece of antique furniture
a ceremonial sword
or else – an ancient tribal chief
a hungry hairy brute
a Himalayan mountain pass . . .

No, just a tiny fruit!

Dictionary Poem

The definition:
> Webs of small spiders
> light filmy substance
> floating in calm air
> or spread over grass
> flimsy threads
> of delicate gauze.

The derivation:
> Gossamer
> goose-summer
> St Martin's summer
> early November
> when geese are eaten
> it being most seen then.

37

Water Flowers

'Place in a fingerbowl'
the packet said.
So we dug out a cracked glass dish,
loosened their paper bands
and dropped them in.

We waited
for the action to begin.

First
they trembled
remembering home,
then shook themselves
unwinding scorpion stings.
From flimsy strings
with fierce fragility
bobbed small gaudy balloons,
cells under microscopes
or lilies on a lake below a bridge.
Some sprouted tassels,
electric pink and blue,
little water-kites
flying in an old bowl
or in a cherry-blossom patterned sky
against high mountains.

We left them to dream
pillowed as painted girls
whose paper walls
enclose their fantasies.

Tricky Situation

Sister Jean likes
sticking on stamps –
she gives them lots of licks!

Brother Mike's
not half so keen –
he'd sooner be stamping on sticks!

What's Reddish?

What's reddish? – a radish,
a fox with his long brush,
a tin of floor polish,
the sky when the clouds blush.

Sausages

How many sides has a sausage?
That's always bothered me.
Some people only grill two sides,
I like mine done on three.

Does that make them triangular?
Nobody really knows.
Some bend themselves into an L,
They're learners, I suppose.

We prick and stab and spear them,
Then the beasts counter-attack
And split their skins, escaping
Like Houdini from a sack.

Some sausages get overcooked,
Some only lightly tanned.
They're just like human sausages
That sizzle on the sand!

Silly Question

'Why is your pram full of holly?
There should be a baby inside.'

'My baby is noisy and smelly
And the holly's enjoying the ride.'

41

Mother's Pets

My mother hates cleaning the budgie,
She says it's her least favourite chore.
Because I'm his owner (in theory)
She reckons I ought to help more.

She tries to shirk walking our spaniel,
It plays up her varicose veins.
She looks such a sight in her wellies
And Dad's anorak when it rains!

She even objects to the goldfish
I won at the school Summer Fayre.
His bowl looks so murky that sometimes
I check to make sure he's still there.

It's not that Mum's cruel or nasty
To animalkind as a rule . . .
But maybe I'd better not mention
These gerbils I've borrowed from school!

What I Saw in London

I saw the Houses of Parliament
where wise laws are made.

I saw the British Museum
full of priceless treasures.

I saw Harrods' Food Hall
with delicacies from all over the world.

I saw the man sleeping in the subway
litter strewn all around him.

I saw the teenage beggar in a doorway
whose sign said 'Homeless. Hungry. Help me.'

I saw the old woman with a striped carrier bag on her
    head
scuttling sideways like a crab.

Warning Signs

BEWARE OF THE DOBERMANS.
Should it be Dobermen?
Take care the Bogeymen
don't get you!

TRESPASSERS PROSECUTED.
Persecuted. Executed!
If they find plants uprooted
they'll get you!

CLOSED CIRCUIT VIDEOS.
Invidious. They're hideous!
Big Brother's barmy if he's
watching you!

Caterpillar Conversation

ILLAR.

Illar.

AT ERP?

Ar.

ER ILL?

Terp.

ATTER?

Cat pill.

AT ER AT, LAR.

Ca, pil.

TER AR.

Ter ar.

Song of the Monkey Brand

Come, housewives, buy your Monkey Brand
And scrub your paint like new.
It cleans your baths and pots and pans,
Your windows and stair-rods too!

    Three jolly factory girls are we,
    Dolly and Ethel and May.
    The hours are long and the pay is poor,
    But we stand all day on the factory floor
    As we work on the Monkey Brand.
    It brightens your home like a baby's smile –
    Your favourite Monkey Brand!

Come, firemen, buy your Monkey Brand
And polish your lamps of brass.
Your engines and extinguishers
Will be clear as a looking-glass!

    Three jolly factory girls are we,
    Nelly and Elsie and Flo.
    We work in Soapery Number Four
    And we stand all day on the factory floor
    As we pack up your Monkey Brand.
    It's better than oil or bathbrick –
    Economical Monkey Brand!

Come, tradesmen, buy your Monkey Brand
And keep your bicycles bright.
It revives your putty scrapers,
Gives your razor strops a bite!

Three jolly factory girls are we,
Sally and Fanny and Vi.
Our coughs are dry and our hands are sore,
But we stand all day on the factory floor
In the dust of the Monkey Brand.
No possible injury can result
From versatile Monkey Brand!

Come, ladies, buy your Monkey Brand
For the shiniest silver in town.
It's used on the palace teaspoons
And His Majesty's golden crown!

Three jolly factory girls are we,
Lottie and Beattie and Lil.
The rot has got our lungs for sure,
But we stand all day on the factory floor,
For you must have your Monkey Brand.
For purity and excellence
You can't beat Monkey Brand!

Come, soldiers, buy your Monkey Brand
And shine your helmets of tin,
Your guns and swords and harnesses
And the medals you're bound to win!

Three jolly factory girls are we,
Mattie and Lizzie and Kate.
Of late there's been some talk of war
And no need of us on the factory floor
And the end of Monkey Brand –
But you'll never win a war without
Four penn'orth of Monkey Brand!

Children of Frost

Children of frost
children of snow
a long way to go to Bethlehem.

        Children of dust
        children of sun
        the star told us to run to Bethlehem.

Out of the frost
out of the snow
we've brought a little fir tree to show to him.

        Out of the dust
        out of the sun
        we've brought a baby camel to bow low
        to him.

Holly sprigs
snow-laden twigs –

        baskets of figs in our arms –

a sheet of ice
edelweiss –

        clusters of dates from our palms

        cardamom and cloves
        lemons from our groves –

sweet herbs to strew on his hay –

some coral beads
pomegranate seeds –

a rainbow we met on the way!

Mary, come,
show your son
to all the children in Bethlehem.
Hold him high,
let him see
all that our love can give to him.

Looking Forward

The days are getting longer.
From my first-floor window
I can sit and watch
the tide of people ebb and flow.
I know them all
the early-morning milkman
postman
paperboy
the schoolchild
worker
shopper.
I invent their lives.
Now I have started looking forward
to the sights and sounds
of summer evenings
by my open window
children playing late
lawnmowers
couples walking dogs.
And yet
perhaps this summer I shall not be here.
My days are getting shorter.